Earthworms

UNDERGROUND FARMERS

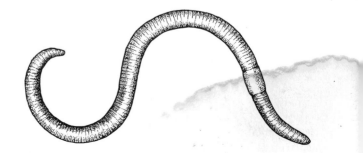

Here's a list of other nonfiction Redfeather Books from Henry Holt

Alligators: A Success Story
by Patricia Lauber

Caves!: Underground Worlds
by Jeanne Bendick

Exploring an Ocean Tide Pool
by Jeanne Bendick

Frozen Man
by David Getz

Lighthouses
by Brenda Z. Guiberson

Great Whales: The Gentle Giants
by Patricia Lauber

*In Search of the Grand Canyon:
Down the Colorado with
John Wesley Powell*
by Mary Ann Fraser

Salmon Story
by Brenda Z. Guiberson

Snakes: Their Place in the Sun
by Robert M. McClung

*Spotted Owl:
Bird of the Ancient Forest*
by Brenda Z. Guiberson

Available in paperback

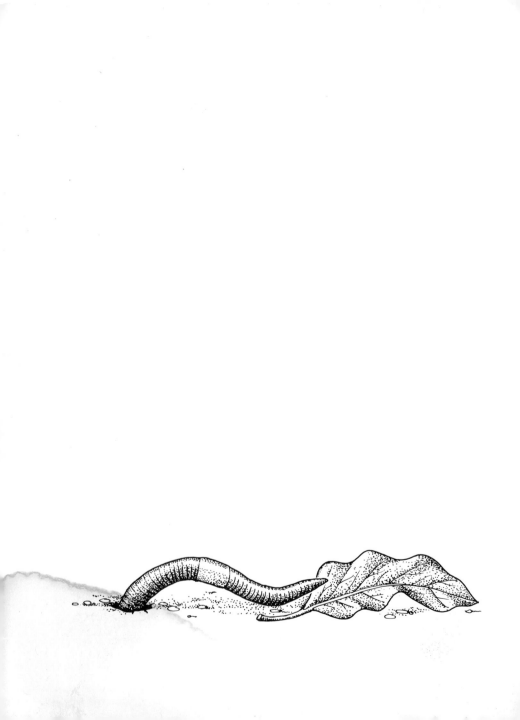

~ Patricia Lauber

Earthworms
UNDERGROUND FARMERS

illustrated by Todd Telander

A Redfeather Book

HENRY HOLT AND COMPANY · NEW YORK

Henry Holt and Company, Inc. / *Publishers since 1866*
115 West 18th Street / New York, New York 10011

Henry Holt is a registered
trademark of Henry Holt and Company, Inc.

Published in Canada by Fitzhenry & Whiteside Ltd.,
195 Allstate Parkway, Markham, Ontario L3R 4T8.

Library of Congress Catalog Card Number: 93-79784

First Edition—1994

Printed in the United States of America
on acid-free paper. ∞

ISBN 0-8050-1910-3
10   9   8   7   6   5   4   3   2
ISBN 0-8050-4897-9
10   9   8   7   6   5   4   3   2   1

Permission for the use of the following photographs is gratefully acknowledged:
page 2 © Runk / Schoenberger, Grant Heilman Photography Inc.
page 8 © courtesy of the Australian Information Bureau
page 12 top © Oxford Scientific Films, Animals Animals / Earth
Scenes; bottom © Zig Leszcynski, Animals Animals / Earth Scenes
page 16 © Dwight Kuhn
page 22 © Ken Highfill, Photo Researchers Inc.
page 28 © Alan Blank, Bruce Coleman Inc.
page 34 © J. M. Labat / Jacana, Photo Researchers Inc.
page 44 © Ted Levin, Animals Animals / Earth Scenes

This book is based in part on an earlier book by Patricia Lauber,
Earthworms, Underground Farmers (Garrard Publishing Company, 1976).

Contents

Earthworms
UNDERGROUND FARMERS

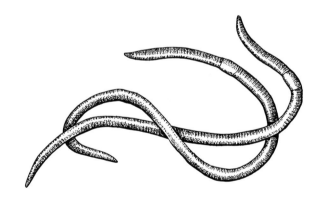

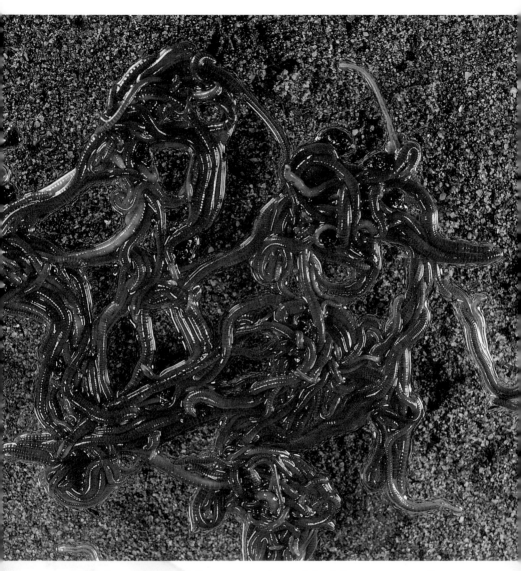

Most earthworm farmers raise a kind known as red wigglers.

A Farm of Worms

*N*ear *Boston, Massachusetts*, there is a farm with no land. It has no vegetables, fruits, flowers, or herbs; no chickens, cows, horses, or sheep. During most of the year, the owner does his farming in the garage. When he goes to New Hampshire for the summer, he takes the farm along.

This odd-sounding farm is an earthworm farm. The worms are raised in sturdy wooden boxes that can be moved about.

The farm's owner, a man named Harry, is one of a number of people who raise earthworms.

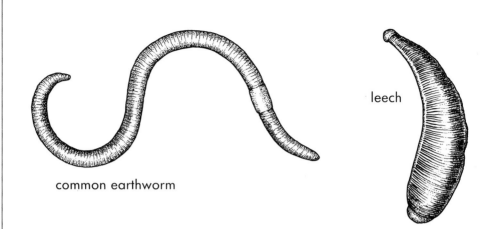

leech

common earthworm

The World's Worms

The world has a surprising number of worms—about 40,000 kinds. Scientists arrange them in big groups—flatworms, roundworms, horsehair worms, hookworms, segmented worms, and others. A segmented worm has a body that is made up of many little rings, or segments.

There are 8,500 kinds of segmented worms. If you swim in ponds, lakes, or rivers, you may have met a leech. It is a segmented worm. Nereids are segmented worms that live in the seas. Some are colored yellow, blue, green, or red. And then there are red wigglers and garden earthworms. They, too, are segmented worms.

The world is home to about 2,700 kinds of earthworms. A few kinds live in lakes and ponds. Most live in the soil. The different kinds may be brown, purple, red, blue, green, or light tan. They also range greatly in size. The smallest are tiny, inch-long worms, while Australia has earthworms that may grow to be 12 feet long and weigh a pound and a half. But most of the earthworms you see are only a few inches long.

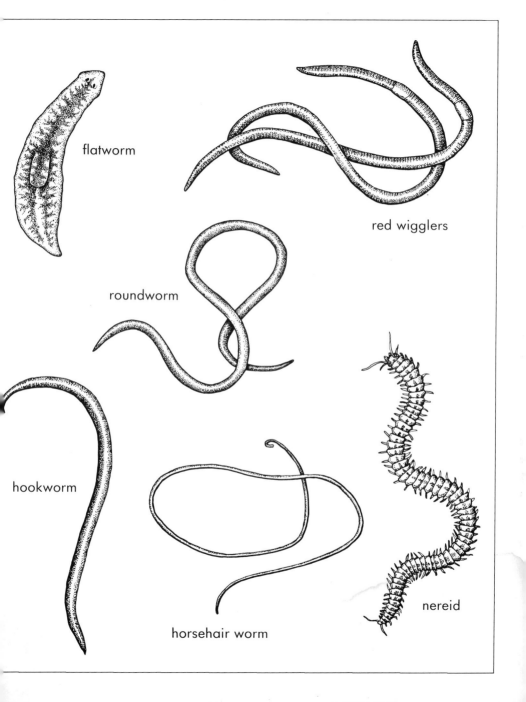

flatworm

red wigglers

roundworm

hookworm

horsehair worm

nereid

Their farms are found from Maine to California and from Texas to Ontario. A big one may have five acres of outdoor pits. A small one may be simply a box in someone's backyard.

Like most earthworm farmers, Harry raises a kind known as red wigglers. They are also known as manure worms, because they are at home in the waste droppings of farm animals. They are at home, too, in garbage made of food wastes. They are at home in garden wastes, such as dead leaves and grass trimmings. All these wastes are food for red wigglers.

As a wiggler feeds, its body breaks down plant and animal wastes. The worm's own droppings form a kind of rich soil. And that is the chief reason why people raise earthworms in their backyards, cellars, and garages. They use their worms to turn waste into something that is good for vegetable and flower gardens. Some also sell worms to fishermen. Some sell worms to other people who want to raise red wigglers.

The owners of big earthworm farms may sell soil to greenhouses and plant nurseries. But mostly they sell worms to people who want to raise them.

Outside earthworm farms, red wigglers live in manure piles and in the litter of leaves and other dead matter on forest floors—wherever there is plenty of food. They are not the kind of earthworms you are likely to dig up in a garden. Most garden soil does not have enough food for red wigglers. But these worms are close relatives of the common garden earthworms, and the two groups are alike in many ways.

The giant earthworms of Australia have the same body plan as their small relatives.

2

An Earthworm's Body

Earthworms all have the same body plan. Look closely at one and you will see that its body is made up of many little rings, or segments, with grooves between them. Most of the common earthworms have 100 to 200 segments.

The body is long, slender, and soft. It is soft because an earthworm has no bones. Neither does it have a hard outer shell, the way an insect does.

At first glance it is hard to tell the front end from the back. The ends look alike because an earthworm has no eyes, nose, or ears. It does have a

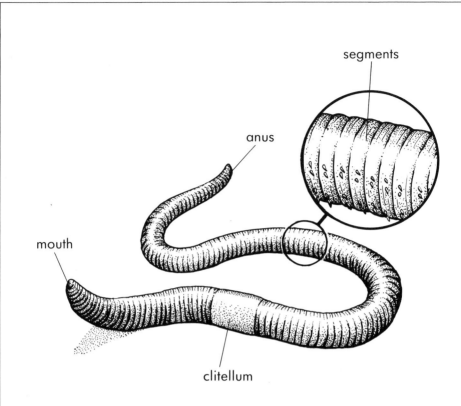

segments

anus

mouth

clitellum

An Earthworm's Body

An earthworm's body is soft and slender, with no bones and no legs. The mouth is a small opening in the head. An opening in the tail is called the anus (AY-nus). It is an outlet for wastes. The body has 100 or more segments, or rings. In adult worms a whitish band called the clitellum covers several segments.

Tiny bristles grow in pairs from a worm's segments. They help the worm wriggle along or anchor itself.

mouth, which is an opening in the first segment. But the mouth may be hard to see.

If an earthworm is wriggling along, it's easy to see which is the front end. It goes first. But there is still another way to tell. An adult earthworm has a whitish band that covers several segments. It is called the clitellum (klih-TELL-uhm). The clitellum is much nearer to the head than to the tail.

To wriggle along, an earthworm uses two sets of muscles.

One set is made up of short muscles that circle the body. Each segment has one of these muscles. When they tighten, the body becomes longer and thinner. The front end pushes forward.

The second set runs lengthwise along the body. When the long muscles tighten, the segments are pulled close together again. The body shortens and swells.

The worm wriggles by stretching itself thin and then pulling its body together. It helps itself along by gripping the soil with tiny bristles that grow in pairs from its segments. The worm can turn the

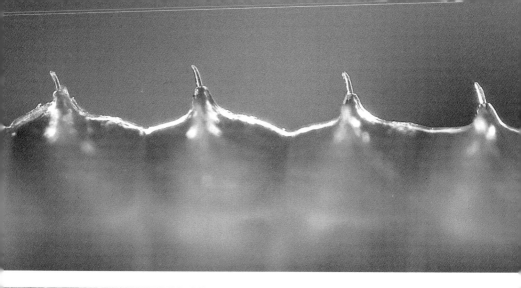

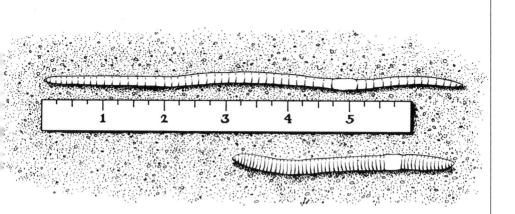

How Long Is an Earthworm?

The answer to this question depends on what the worm is doing. To wriggle along, an earthworm tightens its short muscles—making its body long and slim—and then tightens its long muscles—making its body short and fat.

bristles in any direction. It can pull them in or push them out.

When you handle an earthworm, you can feel

UPPER LEFT: Tiny bristles (shown here much enlarged) grow from a worm's segments. They help the worm wriggle along or anchor itself.
LOWER LEFT: The white band called a clitellum is close to the front end of an earthworm.

that it is slightly slimy. The slime helps the worm to wriggle smoothly through soil. It also does something far more important. The slime allows the worm to breathe.

Like us, earthworms need to take oxygen from the air. The cells of the body need oxygen to do their work.

In our bodies, air is drawn into the lungs. The walls of the lungs are moist. Oxygen dissolves in the moisture, much as sugar dissolves in water. The oxygen then passes through the walls of the lungs into the bloodstream and the heart pumps oxygen-rich blood to all parts of the body.

An earthworm has no lungs. Instead, it breathes through the whole surface of its body. That is why the surface must be moist. Oxygen dissolves in the moisture. It passes into the body and the bloodstream.

An earthworm's body is kept moist by glands in the skin. The glands give off a thick liquid called mucus. The mucus is what feels slimy.

Even with its coating of mucus, an earthworm needs damp surroundings. Without dampness, the mucus dries up and the worm can no longer take in oxygen. That is why earthworms cannot live in very dry soil. That is why they cannot live in sunlight. They need damp, dark places—underground tunnels, or burrows.

Although they do not have eyes, earthworms can sense light. They always wriggle away from it, if they can. Dug up by a gardener's fork, an earthworm hurries back underground.

Earthworms are most likely to come to the surface at night. They may surface to feed or to move to a new area. They also surface to mate.

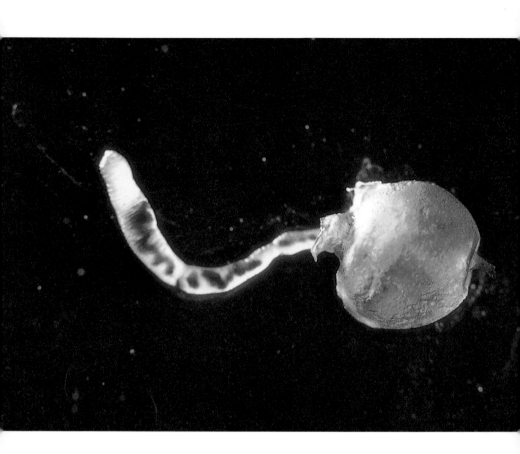

A young earthworm wriggles out of its tiny cocoon.

3

Worms and More Worms

With the animals we know best, a male and a female must mate in order to reproduce, to make young like themselves. Each produces something that is needed to make their young. The female produces special cells called eggs. The male produces sperm cells. When a sperm cell unites with an egg, the egg is fertilized. It can then develop into a young animal.

Earthworms are different. Each earthworm is both male and female—each produces both sperm and eggs. But most kinds of earthworms cannot fertilize their own eggs. Instead they must mate.

Sperm from each mating worm fertilizes the eggs of the other.

In each worm, sperm and eggs are given off through openings in the front end of the body. The openings lie between the clitellum and the head. When mating, worms bring their front ends close together, with their heads pointing in opposite directions. Both worms give off mucus, which holds them together.

Each worm gets sperm cells from the other. These cells are stored in little hollows near the worms' heads. Each worm also gives off egg cells, which are stored in other hollows. When they have finished mating, the worms separate.

A day or so later each worm begins to make a cocoon. Its clitellum gives off a liquid that hardens into a tube. The worm moves backward, drawing the tube over its head. The tube picks up a few egg and sperm cells. Another tube forms, then another, until all the egg and sperm cells are used up.

Once a tube is off the worm, its ends close up. The tube has become a cocoon. Among garden earthworms a cocoon is the size of a grain of rice

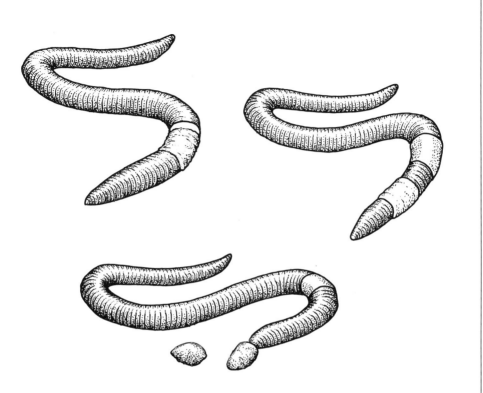

Making a Cocoon

Earthworms may take an hour to mate. Then they separate. Later each worm begins to make a cocoon. Each clitellum gives off a liquid that hardens. The hardened liquid forms a tube around the clitellum. The worm moves backward, sliding out of the tube. As the tube passes over the earthworm's body, it picks up several egg and sperm cells. Once the tube is off the worm, its ends close—it has become a cocoon.

and has the shape of a tiny lemon. Inside the cocoon are the eggs and the sperm that will fertilize them. Earthworms leave their cocoons lying in the soil.

If the weather is mild and the soil is moist, young worms develop in two to three weeks. If the weather is hot or cold or dry, they take longer. Usually two to four young develop in a cocoon. When they first wriggle out, they look like tiny bits of white thread. In a few hours their skins turn dark and they look like small earthworms.

When a worm is three or four months old, its clitellum appears. The earthworm is now old enough to reproduce.

It is hard to say how long earthworms live. When raised by people, they may live several years. But in fields and forests they probably do not live much longer than a year or so. They may drown or be trapped in sunlight. They may be killed by cold or by garden pesticides. Most of all, they may be eaten. Earthworms are food for many animals.

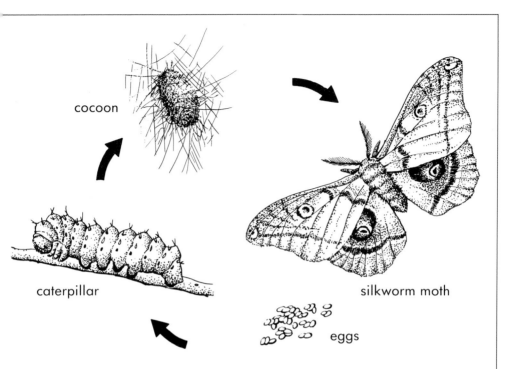

cocoon

caterpillar

silkworm moth

eggs

Worms and Non-worms

When worms reproduce, the young look like small adults. From start to finish, a worm looks like a worm.

Many other small creatures, however, do not come out of their eggs looking like their parents. Instead, they look something like worms and are often called worms—even though they aren't. In time, they will change their form and become like their parents.

The "worm" that you might meet in an apple is really a caterpillar, a young form of the codling moth. The one that ate a hole in your sweater will become a clothes moth. A glow-worm is the young form of a female firefly. Inchworms and silkworms become moths. A mealworm becomes a beetle.

Salamanders are among the animals that eat earthworms.

4

The Worm-Eaters

*M*any kinds of birds eat earthworms. But first the birds must find the worms at or near the surface.

By day earthworms are most likely to come up during a rain. No one is sure why this is so. Perhaps the rain floods them out of their burrows. Perhaps the water keeps air—and oxygen—out of the soil. Perhaps they come up simply because the surface is wet and the air is damp. After a heavy rain you may see hundreds of earthworms on a lawn, driveway, or sidewalk.

On nights when the air is damp and cool, earthworms come out of their burrows. They move about, seeking new areas to live in. With the coming of dawn, they disappear into the ground again.

One common garden earthworm, the night crawler, comes up at dusk or at night to find food. Usually this worm leaves its hind end in the burrow. Its front end stretches out and searches for a leaf or other plant material. The worm can tell one kind of leaf from another, and it chooses the kinds it likes best. Given the choice, for example, it may take birch leaves rather than beech. A night crawler does not feed at the surface, but pulls its food into its burrow.

Sometimes a searching worm is seen by the sharp eyes of a bird. In a flash the bird grabs the worm. A tug-of-war begins.

The bird pulls on the worm. The worm clings to its tunnel. Its long muscles tighten, causing the hind end to swell and fill the tunnel. It anchors itself with its bristles. The bird tugs. The worm hangs on.

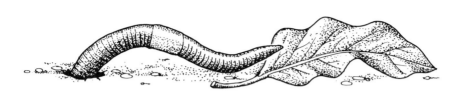

Sensing the World

Earthworms are very simple animals. They cannot see, hear, or smell things. But they can find out what they need to know by sensing the world around them. They can tell whether a place is light, damp, or dry. They can tell one kind of food from another.

Earthworms do not have eyes, but they can sense light through groups of nerve cells in their skin. Most of these cells are near the front end of the body. Earthworms seem to sense light much as we sense heat—we do not see heat, but we feel it. They always move away from bright light toward dim light or darkness, unless the light is red. They do not sense red light.

That is why scientists may study earthworms under red light. The worms stay still, instead of wriggling away, yet the scientists can see them. Fishermen in search of bait may use a red light to look for worms at night. But the fishermen must walk softly. Earthworms have no ears and cannot hear, but they can feel the ground shake.

Earthworms have a good sense of touch. They feel their surroundings through nerve endings in their skin. They can tell if a place is damp or dry, rough or smooth. They can find a crack where they can hide from light.

Earthworms also have a sense of taste. Experiments show they have favorite kinds of leaves and also that there are kinds they will not eat at all.

Sometimes the bird wins and flies away with the worm. Sometimes the worm escapes. And sometimes the worm is torn in two. The bird gets part of the worm, but part remains.

If the bird gets a big piece of worm, the remaining part dies. If it takes only a few segments, the worm will probably live. A worm can grow new segments at either end of its body to replace any it loses.

Underground an earthworm is safe from birds. But it is not wholly safe. Burrowing animals hunt and eat large numbers of earthworms.

One of these animals is the shrew, a tiny mammal with a huge appetite. To stay alive, a shrew must eat at least once an hour. It eats about three times its own weight in food every day. It will eat almost anything it finds—seeds, snails, and grasshoppers, as well as birds and snakes far larger than itself. But earthworms make up a big part of its diet.

The mole is another earthworm hunter. Moles burrow through the ground both to make a home and to find worms and insects. Earthworms are one of their main foods. In fact, moles may even store earthworms as a winter food supply. They bite off the front ends, taking just enough to keep the worms from growing new segments. A scientist once found about a thousand such worm corpses hung on the walls of a single mole tunnel.

Earthworms are also eaten by toads, skunks, and other animals.

Even so, there are a great many earthworms in the world. And this is a good thing for the world's plants. In nature earthworms serve as underground farmers. As they tunnel, they act as living plows.

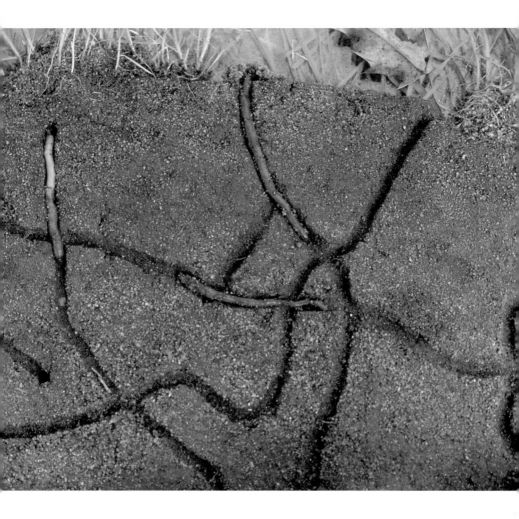

The underground tunnels of earthworms let air and water reach plant roots.

5

Living Plows

*I*n spring, farmers plow their fields. One reason they plow is to loosen up the soil before planting. Well-plowed soil is spongy, with many spaces for air and water to reach the roots of plants.

Crops need soil that has been plowed. So do plants that grow wild—the trees of forests, the grasses and flowers of plains, prairies, and meadows. All have roots that need air and water.

In nature most plowing is done by earthworms. They are living plows, and they are at work in nearly all land areas. The only places they cannot live are ones where the ground is frozen or dry most of the year.

Earthworms exist in surprisingly big numbers. One acre of good land may have anywhere from 50,000 to a million worms. Many kinds live in the top 18 inches of soil, but some kinds burrow down as much as eight or nine feet. As these huge numbers of earthworms tunnel, they loosen the soil.

The way a worm tunnels depends on whether the soil is soft or hard.

Soft soil has many tiny spaces. The worm simply wriggles through them. It stretches thin and wedges its front end into a space. Then it tightens its long muscles. When the body shortens and swells, soil particles are pushed aside. As the earthworm wriggles along, it makes a tunnel. If it meets a stone, it shoves the stone aside. A worm can move a stone that is 50 times its own weight.

Clay and other hard-packed soils do not have little spaces that a worm can wriggle through. It burrows by swallowing soil, making its own space.

Plant roots often follow the easy paths made by earthworms.

A human farmer plows his fields to loosen soil. He also plows to turn over the soil and mix its layers. Plowing brings up soil and minerals from below.

In nature this work is also done by earthworms.

Earthworms swallow large amounts of soil. They swallow some in burrowing. Many kinds swallow more soil as they feed. These worms eat the remains of plants and animals that they find in the soil. As they eat the dead matter, they take in soil.

The soil passes through the earthworm's long body and out the hind end. It forms lumpy little piles called castings. But the castings are not dropped where the worm ate the soil. They are dropped somewhere else, because the worm has moved on. Some worms leave their castings underground. Some leave them at the surface. In this way, earthworms turn over the soil. They mix soil from one layer with soil in another. They bring soil to the surface from below. The earthworms in one

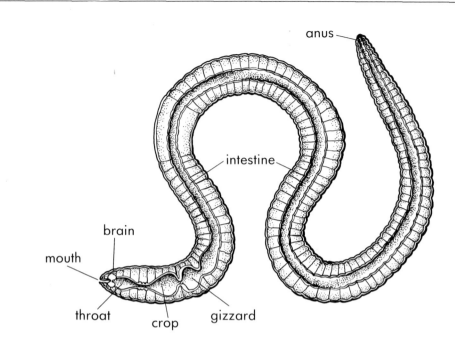

Inside an Earthworm's Body

An earthworm has no teeth, and so it cannot chew its food. It takes food into its mouth. The food is pushed along by muscles in the throat and stored for a short time in the crop. Then it passes into the gizzard, which is made of strong muscles. The gizzard grinds the food, aided by small stones from the soil that the earthworm swallowed along with its food.

When the food is thoroughly ground, it moves on into a long tube called the intestine. There food is digested—broken down by special juices given off by the intestine. Some of the food passes into the bloodstream and is carried to other parts of the earthworm's body. The rest, along with any soil that the worm has swallowed, passes out the hind end through the anus.

acre of land may turn over 40 tons of soil a year.

By tunneling, earthworms loosen up the soil. By swallowing soil, they turn it over. And by feeding on dead matter, they do something even more important. They recycle minerals. They take minerals out of dead matter and put them back in the soil, where plants can use them again.

6

Living Recycling Centers

*F*or good health and growth, people need certain minerals. Three of them are iron, calcium, and potassium. Most of us get our minerals from the foods we eat, although some people buy extra minerals in stores.

Plants, too, need minerals for good health and growth. Their minerals come from the soil and are taken up by their roots.

When a farmer harvests his crops, he is also harvesting the minerals in them. When his crops leave the farm, so do the minerals. They are then used

By feeding on litter, earthworms help to break it down and to release minerals that plants need.

by the people and animals that eat the farmer's crops.

By plowing, the farmer brings up some minerals. But there are not enough of them in the soil to support his crops year after year. So he fertilizes his fields to replace minerals taken from the soil.

Like the farmer's crops, plants in forests and grasslands keep taking minerals out of the soil. No human farmer replaces these minerals. Even so, the soil does not wear out. The reason is that in nature, minerals are recycled. They are taken out, used, and put back—over and over again.

Minerals from the soil are taken up and used by plants. Some of the minerals move on to animals—animals that feed on plants and animals that feed on the plant-eaters. For a while, the minerals remain in the plants and animals. But sooner or later they start on their way back to the soil. They fall to the ground as litter.

Every autumn, for example, trees of the forest shed their leaves. The leaves litter the forest floor. During the year many other kinds of litter are added. There are the waste droppings of animals.

Seeds, petals, fruits, and other plant parts fall to the ground. Branches snap off. Whole trees fall. Small plants die. So do forest animals.

All this litter is rich in minerals from the soil. With the passing of time, the litter rots, or decays. It is broken up. It changes its form and becomes a kind of soil. As this happens, minerals are released and go back into the soil.

But decay does not simply happen by itself. Decay is caused by many small forms of life, such as bacteria, mites, springtails, beetles, millipedes, earthworms. They feed on litter, and their feeding breaks it down. Their feeding releases the minerals in a form that plants can use.

Earthworms are big eaters of litter. In one acre of forest land, earthworms may eat 10 tons of litter a year. In an orchard they may eat 90 percent of the fallen leaves in three months. Earthworms can also eat their way through big leaves. They can eat tough material, such as stems and roots.

Their castings return minerals to the soil. And because earthworms tunnel and move about, they plow the minerals into the soil.

They Cause Decay

Without decay, the earth would long ago have drowned in dead matter. Nothing would ever rot away. But as it happens, dead matter does break down, and its minerals are released to be used again by living plants and animals.

When dead matter breaks down, you can say that it is rotting, or decaying. You can also say that it is decomposing, which means the same thing. It decomposes because it is fed upon by a group of plants and animals known as decomposers.

There are many, many kinds of decomposers. Some are plants and some are animals. The most familiar decomposer plants are fungi, such as mushrooms and toadstools. Unlike green plants, fungi cannot make their own food. Some kinds grow on other plants or on animals and take nourishment from their hosts. Some take their nourishment from dead matter— you often see them growing on dead trees.

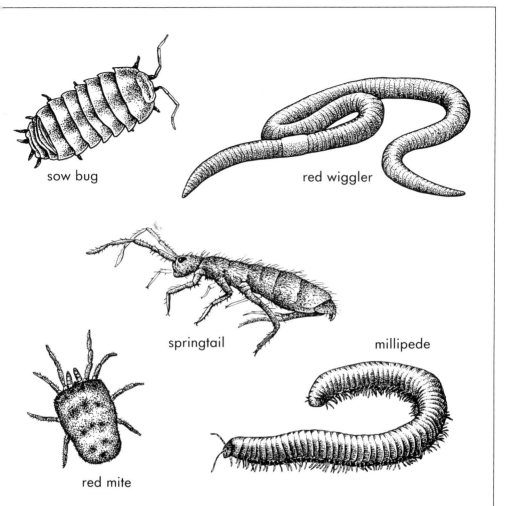

sow bug

red wiggler

springtail

millipede

red mite

Animal decomposers are all small, but if you look sharp in litter or around fallen trees, you will see them feeding. Some of the most common are sow bugs, also known as wood lice; red mites; springtails; and millipedes—a name that means "thousand feet." And, of course, you will find earthworms, probably red wigglers.

Feeding and burrowing, the earthworm goes about its own life. But its way of life is important to green plants, and green plants are very important to all of us.

Among living things, only green plants can make their own food. They are the only things that do not need to eat something else. Using sunlight as energy, green plants make their food by taking carbon dioxide from the air, water and minerals from the soil.

All other living things depend on green plants for food. Some find their food in the plants. Some find their food in animals that eat plants. Some find their food in both animals and plants. But all need green plants.

The green grasses in a field, for example, make their own food. They produce seeds that will grow into new grass. A field mouse may eat some of the seeds, taking its food from a green plant. Later an owl may eat the mouse that ate the seeds. And so the owl depends on the grass as much as the mouse did.

Recycling in Nature

Green plants use energy from the sun to make food out of carbon dioxide, water, and minerals. Parts of the plants are eaten by plant-eaters, which in turn are eaten by meat eaters. When plants and animals die, decomposers turn them into material that plants can use again.

Each year the grass dies back, and in time the owl dies. The forms of life that feed on dead matter—the decomposers—move in. They return minerals to the soil and enrich it. The minerals are used by green plants. Round and round the cycle goes.

Because earthworms play such an important part in this cycle, many people have wondered about harnessing them, about putting them to work. Couldn't earthworms be used to make poor soil better?

The answer is: It depends.

7

Harnessing Earthworms

*I*f land is farmed and not fertilized, the soil wears out. Unless minerals are somehow put back into the soil, few things can grow in it.

Suppose large numbers of garden earthworms were added to such soil. Wouldn't they enrich it with minerals?

The idea has been tested many times, and the tests show that it does not really work. The reason is that poor soil does not hold enough food for the worms. They soon die. As the earthworm bodies decay, they do enrich the soil a little. But the min-

erals are soon used up. The soil becomes as poor as it was in the beginning.

In other words, earthworms alone cannot make the soil richer. To do their work, earthworms need lots of plants making lots of litter.

Sometimes there is new land that has no earthworms. The Dutch, for example, have made land by taking it from the sea. They built dikes to shut out the sea. Then they pumped out the water, worked salt out of the land, fertilized and planted it.

Earthworms can be added to such soil. Suppose fruit trees are being grown. The leaves they drop are food for worms. The worms will plow and enrich the soil—where there are earthworms all green things grow better. But the earthworms must be carefully chosen. They must be a kind that can live in this sort of soil and this sort of climate and that like the sort of food they find. The wrong kind will die.

Vegetables flourish in this garden, where the soil has been enriched with the castings of earthworms.

The best way to harness earthworms is not by adding them to soil but by raising them and adding their castings to soil. That is what many earthworm farmers do.

On the earthworm farm near Boston, Harry fills his wooden worm boxes with several kinds of material. Much of it is free. A riding stable gives him manure in exchange for hauling it away. Harry gets dirt from the town dump. He has his own garden wastes and garbage from the family kitchen—carrot tops and orange rinds, lettuce and cabbage leaves, coffee grounds and eggshells, apple cores, and so on. He buys and adds lime and peat moss. Sometimes he also buys cracked corn.

Harry keeps all this material moist. It is kept warm by the action of bacteria within it. In winter Harry helps to keep the heat inside by covering the boxes.

In woods and fields, earthworms are active for only part of the year. They are quiet in dry, hot weather and in cold weather. But on earthworm farms the boxes and pits are warm and damp the year round. So the red wigglers work all year—

feeding, casting their wastes, and also breeding. In less than a year, 1,000 red wigglers may multiply into one million.

Harry harvests some of his worms and sells them. But mostly he is interested in the worm castings. He harvests these by dumping a box onto a plastic sheet under a bright light. The worms wriggle away from the light to the bottom of the pile.

Harry puts new material in the box. He removes much of what he dumped. The rest, with the worms, goes back into the box.

The castings go into Harry's flower and vegetable gardens. His flowers are the envy of his neighbors. His small garden in New Hampshire yields all the vegetables his family needs. And in time all the vegetable and flower wastes go back into the worm boxes.

Harry is very pleased with his earthworms. Someday soon, he says, he would like to go into the earthworm business. He would like to teach other people how to raise worms. He would like to see more and more rich soil made out of things that people now throw away.

With and Without Worms

Scientists who study crops tried this experiment. Three bean plants were grown in the same soil, with the same amounts of fertilizer, heat, and light. The pot at left had no earthworms. The center pot had dead earthworms, which enriched the soil for a while. The plant in the center pot yielded nearly three times as many beans as the plant at left. The pot at right had live worms and the highest yield. After a while the center plant lost its high yield, but the plant at right did not. It kept on bearing beans and even produced a small second crop. A few worms made a big difference.

An earthworm, Harry says, is not much to look at. It has very little in the way of a brain. But without the tunneling, feeding, and castings of these underground farmers, the world would be a very different place from the one we know.

Index

Page numbers in *italic* refer to illustrations.